Original title:
The Heartbeat of the House

Copyright © 2025 Creative Arts Management OÜ
All rights reserved.

Author: Amelia Montgomery
ISBN HARDBACK: 978-1-80587-104-0
ISBN PAPERBACK: 978-1-80587-574-1

The Life Within the Threshold

Each morning starts with a loud creak,
The cat jumps high, gives quite a squeak.
Coffee brews, the toast is done,
Pajamas dance, oh what fun!

Kids race through, a chaotic blur,
Chasing dreams and a candy stir.
Laughter echoes, spills on the floor,
Life's a party, who could ask for more?

Tides of Togetherness

In the kitchen, pots clash and sing,
A spatula flies, what chaos they bring.
Dancing to tunes on a whim,
The dog joins in, a clumsy swim.

With each meal, stories unfold,
Noodles and jokes, a sight to behold.
Spills and thrills, oh what a show,
Together we dance, let the laughter flow.

Warmth in the Waiting Room

Waiting rooms filled with playful spies,
A cat on the couch, with mischievous eyes.
Magazines stacked, with tales to share,
Comfy chairs, and snacks everywhere.

Each knock on the door sparks laughter bright,
Who will burst in, a surprise tonight?
A joke, a smile, bedtime's near,
In this cozy place, the joy's sincere.

Comfort's Cadence

Socks mismatched, a curious style,
Chasing dust bunnies, all with a smile.
The couch hugs us through thick and thin,
Where games are played and laughter begins.

In every nook, fond memories lean,
Board games stacked, a victory scene.
Tickle fights and stories long,
In this rhythmic space, we all belong.

Balancing Echoes and Silence

In the kitchen, pots start to dance,
With every stir, they take a chance.
The cat gives a look, as if to say,
"Save some for me! It's a buffet!"

In the hall, shoes start a fight,
Sneakers and boots, all day and night.
They tumble and trip, creating a mess,
While I just sit back, not quite impressed.

In the living room, cushions collide,
Pillows rejoice when the kids decide.
They leap and they land, it's a bouncy show,
"Who needs a gym? We're pros, don't you know!"

Upstairs the echo of laughter reigns,
Toys lay in wait for a royal train.
But watch where you step, oh what a scene!
One wrong move and you're part of the routine!

With echoes of giggles and whispers that gleam,
This house spins stories like a wild dream.
So here's to the chaos, the joy that unfolds,
In each silly moment, life's laughter it holds.

The Nest of Nostalgia

In corners where dust bunnies play,
Old socks tell stories in disarray.
A creaky old chair gives a grunt,
The fridge hums tunes of leftovers' hunt.

Pots and pans dance a wobbly jig,
While the clock ticks on, a tad too big.
The wallpaper whispers its faded dreams,
Of picnics and pie, of laughter and screams.

Cadences in the Corners

The curtains sway with giggly grace,
As the spider spins in a lacy space.
The cat takes a leap, all fluff and flair,
While a goldfish watches from a watery chair.

Echoes of voices from days of yore,
Mix with the sounds of feet on the floor.
In this cozy nook, every laugh's a chord,
A tune from the past, on nostalgia's board.

Melodies of Mismatch

Socks collide in a colorful fight,
One stripy, one polka, oh what a sight!
The spoons hold a meeting, a spooner's spree,
While mismatched forks argue, 'let's all be free!'

The quilt on the sofa sings patchwork blues,
While odd mugs laugh in their funky hues.
Every item plays notes of delight,
Creating a symphony, cheerful and bright.

The Carpet's Quiet Story

The carpet whispers tales, so soft and sweet,
Of coffee spills and dancing feet.
It holds the secrets of every visitor's stride,
A plush storyteller, where memories glide.

Under the couch, crumbs gather around,
It dreams of the parties, the laughter, the sound.
A yarn of nostalgia woven with care,
In every stain, a moment's flare.

Rhythm in the Walls

The kitchen hums a jazzy tune,
While pots and pans start to croon.
A fridge that rattles with delight,
In the dance of food, we eat at night.

The floorboards creak a silly song,
As the cat struts by, where it belongs.
With every step, they squeak and moan,
Saying, 'Hey there, you're not alone!'

Echoes of a Sheltered Soul

In the bathroom, splashes and giggles,
As rubber ducks do silly wiggles.
The mirror fogs with laughter's breath,
A little chaos that teases death.

The curtains sway like dancehall queens,
While socks wage war on the washing machines.
Every nook and cranny swells with cheer,
Reminding us, there's no need to fear.

Pulse of the Abode

A heartbeat thrums in the living room,
Where the couch declares, 'Let's consume!'
Popcorn pops, and laughter bursts,
TV blaring, amid our firsts.

Chairs wobble, attempting to groove,
Each family member finds their move.
In this lively, quirky space,
We find joy in the human race.

Whispers Beneath the Roof

The attic squeaks with ghostly fun,
While dust bunnies play hide and run.
Old toys scatter in jovial jest,
Echoing childhood, doing their best.

The chimney coughs with playful smoke,
As squirrels plot and little folk.
Each creak and crack tells tales new,
Of laughter lingering, just like glue.

The Thrum of Tranquility

In the kitchen, pots do dance,
Spatulas and spoons in a prance.
While the cat peers with a sly,
As the water's set to fly.

Coffee brews, it starts to sing,
Cups across the counter ring.
Mom's in pajamas, hair askew,
Sipping joy, with a woo-hoo!

Cadence of Comfort

Shoes piled high by the door,
One's a sneaker, one's a chore.
The dog digs deep in the pile,
Who knew tennis balls had style?

Chairs squeak with a playful tone,
Echoes of laughter have grown.
Dad cracks jokes that make kids yawn,
Still he laughs, from dusk till dawn.

Harmonies of Everyday Life

Morning chores in a silly race,
Toothpaste fights and foam in space.
Dad's on track to miss the train,
With hair like it survived a hurricane.

Dinner's a mix of foods that blend,
Mystery meat on a plate to send.
'This is how my mother made,
But mine's got a twist—don't be afraid!'

Beat of the Family Nest

An oven timer's joyful chime,
Burned cookies, oh, what a crime!
Kids giggle while they steal a bite,
Then dash away, oh what a sight!

Evenings filled with tales and cheers,
Pillow forts and sneaky peers.
Under blankets, whispers float,
In this madness, we all gloat.

The Breath of Belonging

In the kitchen, pots dance with glee,
Dishes sing loud, as we sip our tea.
The fridge hums a curious tune,
While socks hide out, in the cupboard's gloom.

Walls whisper secrets; the dog will chew,
Chairs wobble, shaking off the dew.
Laughter lingers like a stray cat's purr,
In this tiny kingdom, we loudly concur.

Nurtured by the Atmosphere

In the hallway, there's a sock parade,
Each step taken, a new game played.
Pillows argue over who takes up space,
As dust bunnies race for the winning place.

The couch holds tales of naps gone awry,
Remote control battles that make us sigh.
Every corner whispers, 'What's cooking today?'
Echoes of laughter are here to stay.

The Soul Nestled within Four Walls

Under the table, cats plot a coup,
While the popcorn's waiting, all fresh and new.
The clock giggles, hands spinning around,
Tick-tock tickles in this bustling ground.

Lights flicker like fireflies in June,
While the toaster performs its morning tune.
Chairs hiss in comfort, tales to unfold,
This lively tale is a joy to behold.

Unearthed Secrets in Stillness

In the pantry, a cookie jar sighs,
Muffins hold secrets with crumbly ties.
The floor creaks softly with stories untold,
Of mischief and mayhem, both young and old.

The garden looks on with a knowing glare,
As butterflies flutter without any care.
Each window peeks out with a playful glance,
Inviting the world for a whimsical dance.

Stillness Between the Walls

In silence, the couch does squeak,
The fridge whispers secrets all week.
Dust bunnies dance on the floor,
While the old clock snores by the door.

Light bulbs flicker, they seem to play,
Mysterious shadows come out to sway.
The cat in the corner takes a chance,
With a leap and a stretch, she's ready to prance.

Empty dishes start to plot,
The sink chuckles, it's quite a lot.
Towels whisper tales of old,
Napping aside in colors bold.

The Rhythm of Routine

Every morning, the toast pops up,
The coffee's aroma fills the cup.
The dog's excited, doing a jig,
As the cat rolls her eyes, oh so big.

The washing machine takes a spin,
While socks plot revolution within.
Brooms and mops all take a stand,
Forming a band, it's quite unplanned!

Evening comes, the TV's blare,
Remote controls begin to share.
With snacks and laughs, the night rolls on,
While we argue who's right and who's wrong.

The World Within Four Walls

Within these walls, a ruckus thrives,
With mismatched socks and bustling hives.
The dog's popcorn crunch is so loud,
While the cat sits there, so proud.

Dinner prep sparks the chaos anew,
Potatoes are flying, what's left to stew?
The kids' laughter fills the space,
As flour clouds turn into a race.

In shadows, we hear pots and pans,
Complaints from chairs, and teenage plans.
A world so small, yet vast in cheer,
Caught in the laughter we hold dear.

The Ancestral Echo

Grandma's chair still creaks with glee,
As Grandpa's ghost tells tales with tea.
Family photos giggle so bright,
While the blender hums through the night.

Old recipes weave through the air,
While cousin Tim dances without care.
A tapestry of laughter spins,
As history grins beneath our sins.

Echoes of mischief rise and play,
Among the knick-knacks, come what may.
With candles flickering, shadows prank,
In this joyful house, we all give thanks.

The Enchantment of Warmth

The kettle whistles, sings a tune,
While toast jumps high, like a lively loon.
The fridge hums softly, a melodic drone,
As socks get lost in their daring roam.

In corners, the dust bunnies plot and scheme,
While the cat dreams big, pursuing a dream.
The chair creaks loud, declaring a place,
For snacks and laughs, a cozy embrace.

The Sanctuary's Subtle Song

The clock ticks loudly, catching each laugh,
While grandpa snores, crafting his own path.
The phony plant waves, a silent cheer,
As the dog sniffs out where snacks disappear.

The floorboards squeak a tune so bright,
While curtains sway, in the soft moonlight.
A spider spins love notes in its web,
As the whole house grins without a ebb.

Traces of Time Within

The pictures smile, they know the score,
As memories dance through every door.
A chair that wobbles tells its own tale,
Of guests and spills, oh, what a trail!

The rug's worn patches, a map of fun,
Where kids have played, and lovers run.
Each crack in the wall, a whispering friend,
Of laughter echoing that will never end.

Airs of Affection

The air is thick with buttery scents,
While family debates make no intents.
The phone rings loud, with gossip galore,
About auntie's cat who found a new door.

The plants nod gently, taking it all in,
As the floorboards groan, tired of their spin.
Together they laugh, this quirky crew,
In a space so alive, under skies so blue.

Stories in the Shadows

In the corners where dust bunnies play,
Old tales are hiding, oh what a display!
Whispers of mischief from chairs that creak,
Every nook tells a tale, so surreal and unique.

The cat in the corner is plotting again,
With eyes full of secrets from where it has been.
The shadows are giggling, they dance with delight,
As stories unravel through the soft, fading light.

Living Memories of the Porch

On the porch we gather to sip and to chat,
The chairs complain loudly, as if they're all that.
The wind tells a joke that the flowers can cheer,
While the old wooden floorboards creak with a sneer.

Sipping lemonade with a twist of the elbow,
Chasing away bees like a circus haphazard show.
The sun sets with laughter that nudges the stars,
We reminisce about ghosts down at the bazaar.

Echoing Laughter

In the halls of the home where echoes reside,
Laughter rolls out like a bouncing tide.
From the kitchen, the clang of a pot and a spoon,
In fragments of joy, we dance to our tune.

Footsteps of kids chasing dreams through the maze,
Tickling the walls in a zany craze.
Each giggle and snort is a musical note,
A symphony of fun that's bound to promote.

The Glow of Assembled Hearts

In the glow of the evening, we gather as one,
With stories and snacks, we bask in the fun.
The glow of the candles flickers with glee,
Reflecting the warmth of our quirky family.

The dog steals a cookie, the cat claims a lap,
We're tangled in laughter, no room for a nap.
The night wears on softly, like a favorite song,
In the glow of togetherness, where we all belong.

Silhouettes Against the Wall

In the late light, shadows prance,
Dancing with dust, they take a chance.
Mice throw parties, all dressed in gray,
While cats audition for Broadway play.

A fridge hums tunes, off-key but bold,
Conspiring with cupboards of stories untold.
The old clock chuckles, tick-tock in delight,
While plants gossip softly, in whispers of light.

Journals Left Unread

Dusty tomes sit on the shelf,
Letters from me, unread by myself.
Ink spills secrets, trapped in a loop,
While the cat sprawls, guarding the troop.

Papers whisper tales of great glee,
Yet languish in silence, like a lost key.
A coffee cup snores, full of past brews,
As the spoon gently dreams of sweet curfews.

The Stories We Build

In the corners, laughter hangs high,
Each nail a memory, with a wink and a sigh.
Walls lean in, eavesdropping in glee,
Hearing the tales of you and me.

A rug does the cha-cha, with feet of its own,
While cushions conspire, the kingdom they've grown.
Paint peels like secrets, both quaint and bizarre,
While windows are peeking, spying from afar.

The Essence of Together

Mealtime chaos, forks clash and clang,
As stories tumble out with every bang.
Napkins crumple, like stars in a fight,
While laughter erupts in the soft, glowing light.

An apron dons tales of food gone awry,
With stains like memories, oh so spry!
The dishwasher hums a ridiculous tune,
As spoons trade jokes in the silverware moon.

The Embrace of Chill and Warmth

In the corner, socks do dance,
While the cat twirls in a trance.
The heater hums a silly song,
As we slide around, where we belong.

Tea spills like rain on comic strips,
Laughter erupts, we clutch our hips.
The fridge sings tunes of leftovers,
As we debate our culinary endeavors.

Cushions fight a cushy war,
While the giggles seep from every door.
Under blankets, we take the stage,
Improv comedy on every page.

Bills with faces on them grin,
Papers crowding—let chaos begin!
In the warmth, our hearts expand,
In this quirky, joyful land.

The Collection of Echoed Footsteps

In rooms where ghosts of us abide,
Footsteps echo, we cannot hide.
Each creak and rattle tells a tale,
Of spicy snacks and pizza fail.

The hallway voices, high and low,
Remind us of the midnight show.
As squeaky shoes dance on the floor,
Our laughter drowns out every snore.

With each step, a memory's made,
Sock fights and trouble that we've laid.
The echoes map our crazy times,
Of hidden snacks and playful crimes.

Each corner holds a silly stance,
With dance floors formed from circumstance.
To tread these paths is pure delight,
In this collection, we ignite!

Patterns in the Dust

Dust bunnies making secret schemes,
Hover under our wild dreams.
Patterns twist in sunbeams bright,
Shapes that shift in playful light.

Our shoes trek dirt on polished floors,
As crumbs of laughter weave through doors.
Each corner filled with dusty flair,
In the neglect, we find our air.

Time builds castles in the grime,
The vacuum's howl—it's echoing time.
Embrace the mess, we never fuss,
For beauty lies in patterns, thus.

With every sweep, a tale is spun,
Where every failure turns to fun.
Let those specks be treasure found,
In this chaos, joy abounds!

Threads of Tradition

Grandma's recipes take the stage,
A comedy written on every page.
Burnt toast was once a fam'ly treat,
While spice drawers danced to the beat.

Knitting needles click like castanets,
A fabric woven with no regrets.
Each loop and stitch, a giggle passed,
Traditions made, forever cast.

Gravy spills—oh what a sight!
Dinner's almost ready—hold on tight!
With every toast, a tale of yore,
As the family laughs, and requests more.

Coffee cups with tales to share,
Like our hearts, they brew with care.
In our threads, both laugh and sigh,
Life's a quilt, and we can't deny!

The Symphony of Simply Being

In the kitchen, pots do jig,
As the fridge hums a silly gig.
Spoons dance while the oven sings,
Life's a waltz with all these things.

The sofa sneezes with a creak,
While the dog dreams of chasing a streak.
Laughter bounces off the walls,
Echoes of joy in the hallowed halls.

Light bulbs wink, a flirty tease,
Shadows prance with perfect ease.
The clock ticks, a rhythmic cheer,
In this space, we hold dear.

Mopping floors, a slippery slide,
Brooms join in with so much pride.
Every corner, a tale to share,
In this quirky, cozy lair.

Dreams Weave Through the Rooms.

In the living room, dreams take flight,
Cushions plotting a midnight delight.
The carpet giggles with every step,
Whispering secrets while we all prep.

The cat's on the shelf, queen of her throne,
While the spider spins tales all alone.
Pajamas peek from drawers in a heap,
Inviting the night for a slumber deep.

The lamp waves hello with its gentle glow,
As the curtains do a tango in a slow flow.
The walls hum a tune of carefree play,
Encouraging dreams to dance and sway.

Sneaky dust bunnies conspire at night,
Plotting their escape just out of sight.
They giggle and roll, such merry sights,
In a house where dreams spark and ignite.

Whispers of the Living Space

In the hallway, whispers glide,
With tickles and giggles as they hide.
Every nook holds a chuckling gnome,
Creating a laughter-filled, busy home.

The bathroom mirror gives a wink,
As antics unfold in the sink.
Toothpaste battles and bubbles galore,
Who knew hygiene could be such a chore?

Dining chairs share witty banter,
While forks and knives are the grand dancers.
The tablecloth flutters with pride,
In this lively feast where joy can't hide.

Every step hums a playful tune,
As floorboards bounce beneath the moon.
In this creative, cozy embrace,
Lies the mischief of our living space.

Echoes Beneath the Roof

Under the roof, echoes collide,
With mischievous giggles we can't hide.
Walls holding tales of laughter bright,
Every creak a story comes to light.

The attic's secrets chuckle away,
Finding new games in yesterday's play.
A tattered box dreams of being seen,
Where memories dance in playful sheen.

The windows peek with eyes so wide,
Curious what life unfolds inside.
With each beat, this joy we pursue,
Creating a symphony, fresh and new.

Each corner bustling, full of mirth,
Crafting a home, a joyful hearth.
Beneath the roof, love weaves and spins,
In a lively chaos where laughter begins.

Lullabies of the Living Space

In the kitchen, pots tap dance,
Spatulas twirl in a joyful glance.
Fridge hums a tune, soft and sweet,
While the cat purrs, claiming her seat.

Socks are lost in the laundry maze,
Dust bunnies waltz in a twinkling haze.
Chairs creak stories of meals long past,
Every corner echoes of laughter cast.

The sofa's sighs, a comfy throne,
Blankets fold dreams, never alone.
The clock ticks time with a playful beat,
As life unfolds on this lively street.

Here in this space, chaos meets cheer,
With every mishap, there's nothing to fear.
For in these walls, joy finds its blend,
Each moment a melody that will not end.

Tapestry of Echoing Emotions

Walls whisper secrets, soft as a breeze,
Pillows tell tales, bringing us to our knees.
The lamp's warm glow shares stories at night,
While shadows dance, creating pure delight.

The doorbell rings, a puzzling song,
Is it the pizza? It won't be long!
Laughing kids run, spilling their drinks,
Every mishap is more fun than it thinks.

Picture frames giggle, their stories collide,
As family quirks show the love inside.
The rug rolls out for a tumble and fall,
Such is the charm of living's great brawl.

Here kindness blooms in the odd and the strange,
With every mix-up, hearts rearrange.
In this grand tapestry of silly delight,
We weave our laughter, from day into night.

Resonance of Familiar Footsteps

Each morning begins with a shuffle and sigh,
Coffee brews laughter, as kittens fly by.
Socks and shoes in a playful chase,
Who knew kitchen could be such a race?

Echoes of giggles bounce off the walls,
Chasing the mailman, he dodges the calls.
The sound of the vacuum is a wild event,
As dodging it ushers a grand old lament.

Dishes debate on who'll do the chore,
While the remote whispers, "No more war!"
Footsteps ascend, like a waltz in midair,
Life's merry rhythm, oh, how we declare!

In this comical dance, we trip and we jest,
Finding our way through playful unrest.
Every thud and bump sings out loud,
In this crackling space, we take a proud bow.

Chamber of Unspoken Love

In the hall, a sock sits all alone,
And there lies the heart of our cozy home.
The couch, it knows all our silly schemes,
Holding our secrets and half-baked dreams.

The dog's loud snore, a symphony grand,
As we laugh at his odd, orchestrated band.
Cookies burn while we watch the show,
In this sweet chaos, our affections flow.

An unmade bed tells a tale of the night,
Two's cuddled chaos springs to delight.
Every late-night snack, an undercover feast,
This love slice of life, never the least.

Here in this chamber, where madness collides,
We cherish the moments that humor provides.
With joy overflowing, like stories old,
Our hearts find a rhythm more precious than gold.

Pulse of Togetherness

In the kitchen, laughter brews,
Dancing spoons, some silly moves.
The fridge hums a tune so sweet,
While crumbs invite our happy feet.

Coffee spills, a joyful mess,
Who knew cups could cause such stress?
We argue over who is right,
Yet hug it out by candlelight.

Each wobbly chair holds a tale,
Of secret snacks and grand derail.
The family cat steals the show,
As everyone pretends to know.

In this chorus, quirks align,
Where every flaw feels so divine.
Harmony in chaos flows,
Our hearts entwined, that's how it goes.

The Serenade of Shadows

Shadows dance on painted walls,
Chasing each other down the halls.
A ghostly giggle fills the air,
While dad trips over the puppy's lair.

The creaky stairs, a symphony,
Played by feet that dance carefree.
Each thump and bump, a note of fun,
Where everyone is on the run.

Floors that creak like old pianos,
Serve as stages for grand chorales.
The lamp shakes with every shout,
As night reveals what day's about.

In every shadow, stories reside,
With laughter echoing far and wide.
Our quirks are melodies we compose,
In corners where the charm just glows.

Conversations with the Silence

Whispers hide in quiet nooks,
Like unread tales in dusty books.
The toaster pops with secret pride,
While the cat gives the couch a ride.

Muffled talks behind closed doors,
As socks are lost and laughter soars.
We 'shh' the TV for some peace,
Yet giggles pour, they never cease.

Silent moments, so much is said,
Just a glance can turn the red.
In every pause, a story brews,
Of family love in silly views.

Though quiet reigns with its soft charm,
We're weaving chaos, warm and calm.
A symphony of sighs and bliss,
In every whisper, we find our kiss.

Memory's Gentle Resonance

Old photos giggle from the frame,
As memories play their silly game.
A dance by the fridge, a hop on the floor,
Life's playlist is what we adore.

Pasta sauce stains on the wall,
Mark our fights and friendly brawls.
Forgotten toys under the chair,
Tell of battles fought with flair.

Each echo carries a tune so bright,
With every failure, a shared delight.
We laugh at woes that seem so small,
In our home, we rise, we fall.

Bottled moments in glassy eyes,
Reflecting joy, truth, and the skies.
In the garden of memory's glow,
Laughter is the seed we sow.

Soliloquies of Silent Rooms

In corners where dust bunnies play,
A shoe speaks of yesterday's fray.
The fridge hums secrets, quite absurd,
Whispers of snacks, like a gossiping bird.

The toilet's flush, a laugh so loud,
Carries tales of the bathroom crowd.
Each echo is a playful jest,
In silence, the house feels like a fest.

The sofa sighs with its cushions worn,
A haven for crumbs, it's lived and sworn.
It holds the secrets that we still keep,
While the lamp winks in its glowing sleep.

The walls lean in to hear the fights,
While windows crack jokes on starry nights.
Every creak tells tales of the cats,
As they dart like ninjas, or doormat acrobats.

The Breath of Domestic Life

In kitchens, pots are doing a dance,
Sizzling jokes in a saucepan's trance.
A cheerful spatula sings a tune,
While the toaster pops like a cartoon.

The vacuum hums an awkward rhyme,
As it rolls through the living room grime.
Chasing crumbs like a spirited dog,
It swallows the mess, then does a slog.

The microwave beeps, 'I need a break!'
As leftovers term it a 'food mistake.'
But the dishwasher giggles, 'I'm on a spree!'
Cleaning the dishes with glee, oh me!

Each room breathes the laughter of days,
In little quirks, the mundane plays.
Life's a sitcom, absurd and bright,
In our cozy nest, all feels right.

Melodies in the Hallways

Up the staircase, a symphony swells,
The banister hums as it tells and tells.
Each step creaks with a tune so spry,
While shadows dance, oh me, oh my!

The hallway whispers with wall-frame mirth,
Its stories dance like children at birth.
A picture frame hiccups in the light,
'Look how we age!' it laughs in delight.

Behind each door, a melody stirs,
From laughter to sneezes, it cleverly purrs.
The shadows giggle as they glide by,
Creating secret concerts in the sky.

In echoes and whispers, hilarity roams,
With shelves holding the tales of our homes.
A house of rhythm where laughter's encore,
Every corner, a musical lore.

Sanctuary of the Soul

In the quiet, the couch softly snores,
It cradles us through life's open doors.
With coffee cups sharing the gossip and fun,
'This morning was wild, let's do it again!'

The curtains sway in a gentle breeze,
Tickling the cat who sneezes with ease.
A pillow whispers, 'Design me a dream,'
As laughter erupts like whipped cream on steam.

The rug holds footprints of days unplanned,
Where friends convene and antics are grand.
Every grain tells of joy and surprise,
As the bookshelf snickers, 'I see your eyes!'

In this refuge where silliness reigns,
The walls bear witness to shenanigans' chains.
Life spins in circles, with joy as our goal,
In our sanctuary, we uncover our soul.

The Fading Echo of Footfalls

In the hall where echoes dance,
The dog steals socks with a glance.
The fridge hums a silly tune,
As I search for cheese by the moon.

The cat plots on the window sill,
Pondering life with a quiet thrill.
Footsteps fade on the dusty floor,
Wondering what I came here for.

The creaky stairs squeak and sigh,
While the old clock ticks by and by.
Each cartwheel of dust in the sun,
Laughs at all the silly fun.

With every squeak and every creak,
The floors seem to giggle and speak.
In this house of laughter and cheer,
The fading echoes always near.

Lullabies of Lived Experience

In the kitchen, spatulas hum,
While the microwave's a beatbox, fun.
A spoon serenades the open jar,
As the fourth slice of toast flies far.

Pots and pans join the joyful choir,
Cooking mishaps spark a fire.
The blender whirs a grumpy song,
Saying "Hey! You've been here too long!"

Coffee brews with a lovely glee,
While the milk carton begs, "Not me!"
Each sip carries tales of the day,
Lullabies that fade away.

The tea kettle whistles, full of sass,
While crumbs from breakfast make a pass.
In this home, with laughter inside,
Every moment is a fun ride.

Shell of Memory

In the living room, a chair reclines,
Holding secrets, quirks, and lines.
A shell from trips to the bright shore,
Whispers tales of laughter and more.

On the walls, photos hang with glee,
Recording who we've come to be.
Silly poses, goofy smiles,
Capturing moments that stretch for miles.

The couch transforms in such a way,
Becomes a ship on a pretend bay.
Childhood laughter fills the air,
As we dance without a care.

Under blankets, we tell our tales,
Of pirates, dragons, daring gales.
A shell of memory, soft and bright,
In this cozy home of delight.

Soft Tapestries of Life

In the corners, dust bunnies play,
Making mischief throughout the day.
The curtains sway like they have dreams,
Whispering secrets in sunlit beams.

Underfoot, the carpet hums low,
Sharing stories only it knows.
Socks mismatched, a playful sight,
As they giggle in morning light.

Pictures hang, like stories untold,
In vibrant colors, bold and old.
Each thread woven with giggles and sighs,
Creates a quilt where laughter lies.

In this tapestry, soft and bright,
Life's little moments feel just right.
For every stitch, a tale to entwine,
In this house of love, all is divine.

Stirrings in the Quietude

In the kitchen, pots go clatter,
A spoon escapes, it all goes splatter.
The fridge hums tunes folks can't ignore,
While leftovers plot for a grand encore.

Dust bunnies dance under the light,
Chasing each other, oh what a sight!
Socks in the dryer, lost in a game,
They're planning a trip, we can't find the same.

The cat leaps high, just for a thrill,
Crashing the curtain, with flair and skill.
Even the dog thinks it's quite absurd,
When a rogue squirrel fancied a word.

With laughter echoing through the halls,
Every corner whispers, every shadow calls.
In this wacky chaos, love finds a way,
In the stirrings of quiet, we play every day.

Foundations of Affection

Under the stairs, a shoe-clad mess,
My partner just sighs, 'It's love, I guess.'
The table wobbles; one leg on the brink,
Jokes fly around faster than we think.

A portrait askew, oh what a scene,
A masterpiece, or just a routine?
With mismatched chairs, we take a seat,
Every meal's shared, even the sweet.

Spilled juice and laughter make quite a sight,
The dog jumps up, trying to take flight.
In this lovely mess, we find our truth,
Foundations are built with laughter and youth.

A scrabble game turns into a roar,
Every letter's a story, who could ask for more?
Through laughter and mishaps, the love we find,
In our quirky haven, we're perfectly aligned.

Song of the Open Door

The door swings wide, a creaky tune,
Welcoming squirrels and the odd raccoon.
Neighbors poke heads, 'What's the ruckus?'
We shrug and laugh; it's mental circus!

Kids race past, on their bikes they zoom,
In this open air, there's always room.
The invitation's clear, with a playful shout,
'Come one, come all, there's no way out!'

Sunlight spills like a golden stream,
In the garden, the gnomes plot and scheme.
They gossip about the plucky blue jay,
Life's a comedy; join in the play!

Each knock at the door brings a new twist,
Unexpected visits you wouldn't want missed.
With laughter and snacks, the fun's never poor,
In our quirky hive, love's the decor.

Whispers From the Attic

Up in the attic, old treasures hide,
A dusty chair where memories abide.
With cobwebs singing their ancient song,
A family history, both funny and strong.

The trunk of old clothes, so wild and absurd,
An outfit that leaves everyone blurred.
Who wore those pants, such flares of delight?
It's a mystery lost in time's endless flight.

Old toys are talking; they laugh with glee,
Tales of wild summers, just wait and see!
With wooden blocks that tumbled like that,
Life's quite the trip—we're glad for the chat.

As spiders spin tales, we giggle and glide,
In the heart of the home, where laughter won't hide.
Our attic's a stage, where the past joins the now,
With whispers of joy—take a bow!

The Soul's Sanctuary

In the corner, the cat takes a snooze,
While the dog plots on how to steal shoes.
A pot on the stove is bubbling with glee,
While the fridge hums tunes of a cold symphony.

The walls listen close to whispers and cheers,
As laughter erupts, dissolving the fears.
Cookies baking, a war of the treats,
Who will claim victory? The snacking elite!

A sock on the floor is matching its mate,
Their journey together we cannot await.
The sofa's sagging, worn down by the tales,
Of epic adventures and laughable fails.

In every crevice, a story resides,
Of socks that have vanished, of chaos that hides.
This vibrant space, alive in each brush,
Is where love finds rhythm, amidst all the hush.

Pulse Beneath the Floorboards

Tap-tap of little feet dancing around,
The floorboards creak like they're all spellbound.
A vacuum's a monster, invoked in our fun,
The chase is on; the race has begun!

Underneath the couch, a treasure awaits,
Forgotten toys bring back old debates.
What once was a tiger now looks like a goat,
With a smile that seems to use humor as a moat.

Squeaky voices echo from every nook,
As we narrate dramas, our own little book.
The rhythm of chaos, the dance of the night,
Turning mundane moments into pure delight.

So let the music play, let the mishaps roll,
With laughter and prancing, we give it our soul.
In the bass of our giggles, our joys intertwine,
In this raucous concert, our hearts boldly shine.

Fireside Conversations

Gather 'round the fire, we bring stories anew,
Tales of burnt marshmallows, and dreams in the blue.
The flames dance like friends, inviting the night,
While shadows practice their silly fright flight.

"There was once a spoon," says Grandma with a wink,
"That turned into a fork, or so people think!"
Laughter erupts like popcorn on heat,
As grand tales and giggles swirl round like a beat.

The creaky old chair joins in with a squeak,
Violin of memories, just finding its peak.
Pillow fights start, filling air with delight,
As sleep slowly tiptoes, sneaking in from the light.

The warmth of the fire, a hug for the heart,
Filling every moment with laughter and art.
We gather our dreams and our quirky charms,
In these fireside chats, we find all our calms.

The Harmony of Belonging

In a world made of laughter, we strum our own song,
With mismatched socks, who cares if they're wrong?
Each voice a note, blending in a tune,
While the cupcake thief plans his heist by noon.

Pajamas are uniforms; we parade with pride,
The dance of embracing our quirks magnified.
The joy in the mess, the clutter divine,
Where each little chaos is perfectly fine.

A dance of the kitchen, with spatula moves,
As we twirl through the chaos and find our grooves.
'Dinner's almost ready!' becomes a grand show,
With plates full of laughter, and stories to grow.

So here, we belong in a funny brigade,
With antics that sparkle and never will fade.
In a harmony stitched with threads of us all,
We celebrate life's quirks, forever enthralled.

Vibrations in the Living Room

Couch cushions bounce with quiet glee,
A cat navigates like it's on a spree.
The roomba dances, bumping with flair,
Each corner uncertain, nothing can compare.

TV blares while the popcorn flies,
Remote in hand, oh what a surprise!
Children giggle, spilling their snack,
A living room circus, no moment lacks.

Intimacies of the Everyday

Morning coffee brews with a sputter,
The toaster pops with an unfunny mutter.
Socks vanish, but laughter remains,
In this daily dance, no one complains.

Chores become a rhythmic delight,
Broomstick tap-dancing, oh what a sight!
Laundry giggles, spinning with cheer,
A comedy show, right here, my dear!

Cadence of Comfort

Naps on couches pull us in tight,
Blankets and pillows create the right light.
Snacking and snoozing, life's little rhyme,
In our cozy kingdom, we rule our time.

Whispers of laughter fill the soft air,
A ticklish touch, what's under the chair?
Every heartbeat echoes a friendly tune,
Under the same roof, we're over the moon.

Murmurs in the Kitchen

Chop, chop, the veggies play tag,
The pots start dancing, oh what a brag!
Sizzle and pop, a culinary fight,
Sauce splatters happen; what a delight!

Cookies are baking, they rise with a cheer,
Sugar rush giggles, they simply appear.
Spatula shakes like a shivering friend,
In this tasty chaos, there's no end.

Threads of Togetherness

In the kitchen, pots do collide,
Cats on the counter, with nowhere to hide.
As we bicker over dishes and crumbs,
Laughter erupts as chaos becomes.

Socks on the ceiling, a game of toss,
Dad claims the TV, but really, he's lost.
Mom's trying to find her favorite pen,
Amidst all the giggles that never quite end.

Surprises in drawers, like treasures to find,
A broken old toaster that sparks out of line.
We share silly stories, we can't seem to quit,
All together, we fit, like a bonkers old kit.

Even when things seem a little askew,
This madness, it weaves us, a colorful hue.
With every mishap and every loud shout,
Home is a circus; there's never a doubt.

The Dance of Everyday Life

In the morning, we shuffle, we stumble and sway,
Coffee is brewing, but we're late anyway.
To the rhythm of pan clanks, the kids start to cheer,
When breakfast looks like a mountain of cheer.

Dad spins in pajamas, doing a jig,
While socks disappear, oh, where could they dig?
Mom waltzes with laundry, the spin cycle's loud,
As we twirl past each other, a giggling crowd.

The dog joins the fun, chasing our feet,
While cereal flies in a game of 'let's eat.'
The floor's now a stage for our morning ballet,
With memories crafted in a silly display.

Through lunches packed up, and backpacks in tow,
The dance never stops; it just seems to flow.
With smiles all around, in our daily routine,
Life's a delightful, chaotic machine.

Time's Gentle Tapping

Ticking clocks mark seconds, but we're moving slow,
   A cat on the couch is the star of the show.
   The minutes tumble like cookies on plates,
   In a race against toys that never have fates.

Dad forgets where he put his reading glasses,
Mom's lost in a world where each moment passes.
   With kids' giggles echoing, the hours unwind,
   Time's gentle tapping, we're blithely confined.

In the rhythm of chaos, we find our sweet song,
   Playing hide and seek where the cuddles belong.
   Oh, what a sitcom, life's quirks have flair,
   Each frazzled moment is a breath of fresh air.

Like clocks with no hands, we're whirling around,
   In every mad moment, pure joy can be found.
   With laughter like music, dispatching our fears,
We dance through our days, and we help dry the tears.

Murmurs in the Morning Light

Morning light creeping through the window wide,
Birds gossip softly, like friends side by side.
The pancakes are burning while laughter takes flight,
As we stumble through breakfast in morning's soft light.

With socks on the wrong feet, we giggle and stare,
Dad's hair a wild mess, a true morning fair.
The juice spills in colors that brightened our scrimmage,
In this wakeful chaos, we find our own image.

Amid the soft murmurs of sleepy goodbyes,
Mom's list is a riddle, oh, what a surprise!
From lunches to homework, life reads like a book,
In our cozy mess, it's our souls that we've shook.

With heartwarming moments wrapped snug in a hug,
All the mayhem combines us, we're warm as a rug.
Each day an adventure in life's silly chase,
In the mornings we rise, our hearts find their place.

The Imprint of Smiles

In the corners laughter hides,
While the cat plots her next surprise.
We dance through dust and cheer,
As cookies disappear, oh dear!

Socks tossed like confetti fare,
A pie crust burns, we just don't care.
Wiping frosting from our face,
We find joy in this messy place.

Jokes that linger in the air,
Echo through the rooms we share.
Tickles and snorts, oh what a blast,
Memories that surely last.

In shadows where giggles dwell,
We weave tales we'll never tell.
With love and humor as our glue,
The walls sing smiles, just me and you.

Clatter and Calm

Pots clang like a musical show,
While kids chase one another below.
Oven beeps with a cheerful tone,
As dogs hope for a tasty bone.

Laughter spills from room to room,
Mixing with the scent of bloom.
Dishes crash in a daring race,
Yet peace lingers in every space.

Broom twirls like a march parade,
As crumbs escape, we're not dismayed.
A pancake flips with flopping grace,
Sure to land on someone's face!

Through the chaos, smiles abound,
In this joyful, lively ground.
Here's to each joyful shimmy and shake,
Life's delicious in every break.

Warmth Beneath the Roof

Cuddles bounce like jumping beans,
Snuggled tight with silly scenes.
Hot cocoa held in messy hands,
As giggles dance like jazzy bands.

Through the halls stories flow,
Of mishaps and surprises that glow.
Blankets piled in a cozy nest,
Where every nap feels like a quest.

Game nights filled with playful shouts,
Who will win? Mystery sprouts!
Popcorn settles in every nook,
Each face drawn from a lively book.

Beneath this roof, love soars high,
In playful whispers, we fly.
Where hearts flutter and joy ignites,
This warmth is our favorite light.

The Bridge of Time and Space

Sticky fingers on the clock face,
Time detours for our crazy race.
A dance in the hall, a spin and twirl,
Echoes of laughter in a whirl.

The fridge hums with secrets galore,
While snacks find their way to the floor.
Each moment a treasure, each giggle a grace,
We bounce through the day at a merry pace.

Open windows, fresh air zips,
As toes tap out our playful quips.
Under the stars, stories unfold,
Together in moments, worth their weight in gold.

So here's to the mix of fun and cheer,
In this home where memories adhere.
Through the madness, love finds its place,
A joyful dance in our happy space.

Resonance of Familiar Walls

Every creak tells a tale of its own,
The fridge hums along, a monotone drone.
Lights flicker like they're dancing in glee,
While the cat pounces, as stealthy as can be.

The walls have heard laughter, they remember the fun,
From sock-throwing battles to epic food run.
In the corners, old shoes now gather some dust,
But oh, the memories made, oh, they're a must!

The clock ticks away, keeping up the beat,
As the dog snores loudly, a humorous feat.
Walls covered in photos, all smiles and cheer,
Always a chuckle, whenever friends are near.

So here's to our dwelling, this lively retreat,
Where chaos and joy create laughter so sweet.
A cacophony echoing through every room,
In this house of mine, there's never a gloom.

Rhythm in the Quiet Corners

In the quiet corners, there's quite the parade,
Of socks mismatched and plans that we laid.
The table wobbles, a dance it resolves,
While the chair squeaks, like it's solving our problems.

In the study, a cat naps atop open books,
Chasing mice in dreams, giving curious looks.
The dust bunnies tango, a sight to behold,
In a performance that never gets old.

A spoon drops in the kitchen, oh, what a sound!
Like a drummer who's lost, but still all around.
A pot begins bubbling, a gentle refrain,
As I sip my coffee, embracing the mundane.

Every strip of wallpaper holds stories untold,
Of spilled juice mishaps and adventures bold.
So let's gather 'round as the laughter takes flight,
In this funny rhythm, we'll all feel just right.

Pulse of the Hearth

The oven hums softly, a song of delight,
While cookies are baking, they're out of sight.
A whisk clinks in time, with a melody sweet,
As flour clouds dance, a light fluffy treat.

The microwave buzzes like a busy bee,
Reheating the food from last week's spree.
In the center, the table, where stories collide,
With forks and with knives, our laughter can't hide.

A kettle whistles, it's a cheerful alarm,
As the tea brews with charm, it brings such calm.
The candles flicker, sharing secrets in light,
While shadows perform in the cozy night.

So here's to the hearth, where warmth finds its place,
With bickering banter and a feeling of grace.
Each meal shared is a pulse, a beat we all know,
In this fun little haven, our joy always grows.

Heartstrings of Home

A jingle from keys as I stumble inside,
With grocery bags bursting, like a wild tide.
The floorboards protest, they know I'm back,
As I trip over sneakers, oh, what a knack!

The bathroom door squeaks, a tune all its own,
While the mirror reflects all the laughter grown.
Toilet paper tangling like a playful prank,
Making every moment worthy of a laugh tank.

In the living room, popcorn scattered with glee,
During movie marathons, oh, just let it be!
The couch cushions giggle, they're cozy and round,
While laughter surrounds, such a warm-hearted sound.

So here's to the quirks that we all hold so dear,
From echoes of laughter to moments we cheer.
With love in each corner, and joy in each room,
This home is a garden where happiness blooms.

Harmonies of Hospitality

In the kitchen, pots dance and sway,
As spoons engage in a lively ballet.
The fridge hums a tune, oh so bright,
While the toaster pops in sheer delight.

Guests arrive with laughter and cheer,
Spilling drinks, but never a tear.
The tablecloth makes a great cape,
For the dog who dreams of escaping fate.

On the couch, cushions squish like cake,
Each joke and jest feels like a wake.
The clock chimes a wacky refrain,
Reminding us – we do it again!

In the hallway, a shoe hits a door,
Echoes of giggles, just wanting more.
Every crack and creak tells a tale,
Of fun times wrapped in our heartfelt veil.

Secrets of the Sitting Room

The chairs hold whispers of gossip and woes,
While the cat plots where mischief goes.
Under the table, socks make a nest,
A treasure trove of the untried quest.

The lamp flickers, like it's got a joke,
While the curtain decides to give a poke.
Each cushion adorned with crumbs and crumbs,
Revealing the secret of our fun-loving chums.

On the wall, a picture tilts askew,
Captured moments of the old and the new.
The dust bunnies dance with grace divine,
As guests recall what's truly fine.

In this room, the laughter's the glue,
Binding stories, both false and true.
If walls could laugh, they'd surely roar,
For within these spaces, we always adore.

The Essence of Echoing Spaces

In the hallway, shoes left astray,
Whispers bounce, come out to play.
No echo goes unheard, oh no,
As the dog sneezes – a comic show!

The fridge murmurs secrets at night,
While shadows in corners take flight.
Every squeak and creak on the stairs,
Turns a harmless trip into comedic flares.

Under the table where laughter lingers,
A surprise tickle from the feathered fingers.
In this nest of familiarity bright,
We cook up chaos with sheer delight.

The ceiling fan spins tales of yore,
While the chandelier plays show-off galore.
Amidst this charm, we find our way,
Where echoes remind us to dance and sway.

Dim Light, Soft Sounds

In the glow of a bulb that flickers on cue,
We find solace in moments so few.
The soft sounds of creaking, quite a delight,
Whispers tales of our late-night plight.

The fridge's hum becomes a calming tune,
As the moonlight spills across the room.
In shadows, the giggles begin to rise,
Painting our dreams with infinite sighs.

Under the blanket, a secret exchange,
A stash of candy feels quite strange.
With each crinkle, the laughter grows,
As we dive deeper in cozy throes.

So dim that light, let soft sounds play,
In this warm embrace, we dance away.
Within these walls, we craft our bliss,
For in every whisper, we find our kiss.

Twilight's Soft Serenade

In the kitchen pots start to dance,
The fridge hums a tune, a jolly romance.
The cat struts around like a silly queen,
While the toaster pops toast as if it's a scene.

Chairs creak in joy, they join in the fun,
Baking cookies like they're on the run.
The clock ticks a joke, its hands wave with glee,
As the dog takes a nap, dreaming of a spree.

Windows wink softly at the night sky,
The moon laughs along, oh my, oh my!
Laughter erupts as shadows take flight,
In this cozy abode, everything feels right.

Neighbors join in for a sudden jam,
With pots for percussion, oh what a slam!
Twilight sings softly, in a giggly spree,
Our little home's heartbeat, forever carefree.

Patterns of Light and Shadow

In the living room, the lamp starts to wiggle,
Casting shadows that giggle and jiggle.
The couch tells a secret, it's cozy and bold,
As the carpet spreads whispers, stories unfold.

Dancing beams of light play on the wall,
The clock makes a joke, 'I'm always on call!'
A spider spins webs like a crafty old pro,
While the dust bunnies party, with nowhere to go.

Windows laugh warmly, letting the sun in,
As the curtain flutters, like a cheeky grin.
Footsteps tap lightly, a rhythm begins,
As laughter erupts, oh the joy never thins.

In this house of delight, positivity reigns,
Where the echoes of fun linger just like sweet grains.
Patterns of joy merge in whimsical glow,
In this vibrant home, there's always more to show.

Love's Gentle Pulse

Every heartbeat echoes within these four walls,
The laughter rings out, oh how it enthralls.
Found socks do a tango on the living room floor,
As the fridge spills its secrets: "There's always more!"

Families gather, a mishmash of grace,
With pillow fights happening all over the place.
Love bounces around like a kid on a swing,
Even the goldfish seems to join in the zing.

The blender hums loudly, a melodious tune,
While the microwave chats like a old dancing goon.
With goofy antics, and smiles to share,
This lively abode, joy is everywhere!

In the heart of the home, amidst all the cheer,
The pulse of togetherness keeps drawing us near.
As notes of affection fill every small nook,
Love thrives as we write our own silly book.

Canvas of Conversations

Brushstrokes of laughter adorn every space,
In this lively abode, not a moment we waste.
The walls hold stories, in colors so bright,
They whisper sweet nothings when we turn off the light.

The table is a canvas for meals and for talk,
Where silly debates arise with every snack clock.
The chairs spill their secrets, with giggles and grins,
As the dog licks his paws, contemplating his sins.

With every tick-tock, the clock hums along,
Creating a rhythm, like a joyous song.
Each corner is filled with a map made of smiles,
In this gallery of love, we're all in for miles.

As dusk paints the sky in shades of delight,
Conversations bloom like stars in the night.
With humor our palette, we create every day,
This home is our canvas, come what may!

Life's Cadence in the Corner

In the corner, the cat takes a snooze,
As the clock ticks on, singing its blues.
The fridge hums a tune, slightly off-key,
While the dog dreams of treats under the tree.

The kids race through, laughter so loud,
Each footfall a beat, daring the crowd.
A dance of socks in the living room light,
Who knew chaos could sound so polite?

The microwave beeps, it's dinner time fair,
Popcorn pops wild, filling the air.
With every whoosh and every cheer,
Our joy is a rhythm that's perfectly clear.

In this cacophony, we find our delight,
A family ensemble, both silly and bright.
Life's little sounds, they never do tire,
In the corner, our laughter's the choir.

Heartstrings of Home

A tug at the fridge, a pull at the rug,
Dad's curled up tight with a bug in his mug.
Mismatched socks dance in the hallway so free,
As brother just coughs, says, "That's not me!"

Mom's stirring the pot, gives onions a glare,
While sibling alliances split up the chair.
A spoon takes a dive, the dog makes a dash,
He knows that the crumbs are worth any clash.

The toaster's a drama with bread doing flips,
Each pop sounds like magic, we don't need scripts.
An orchestra swells from the chaos of play,
With every small moment, we find a new way.

Through giggles and humbles, we stumble along,
Crafting our symphonies, somehow they're strong.
The heartstrings vibrate with each silly call,
And this is our music, it's home after all.

Vibrations of the Hearth

The kettle whistles, a shriek and a cheer,
It's tea time, folks, put down that weird beer.
A clattering spoon joins the chorus quite loud,
While shadows move quick, it's a puppet-like crowd.

Dad's slippers are marching, they've lost their parade,
While Mom dances gingerly, avoiding the spade.
The floor squeaks a tune, rhythm's off but still right,
Every tick of the clock seems to brighten the night.

A dog sneezes loudly, shaking the gloom,
The kids giggle soft as the dust starts to bloom.
The warmth of our hearth is a tune of its own,
A raucous orchestra, never alone.

With each little sound, we build our own song,
A lovely, loud anthem where we all belong.
In every wild moment, the laughter takes flight,
In this house, full of chaos, our hearts feel just right.

Sanctuary's Silent Symphony

In the hallway, we tiptoe, playing it cool,
While cats plot their pounce, oh, what a fool!
The couch seems to giggle, all worn and frayed,
As Grandma recounts tales in the sunlight's shade.

We gather 'round tables, both messy and grand,
With stories that rattle like maracas in hand.
The chorus of forks and soft butter's spread,
Each bite is a note, with laughter ahead.

A sneeze breaks the silence, like jazz on a whim,
And suddenly, all eyes on the curious hymn.
The plants sway in rhythm, a dance of the green,
While Goldfish in bowls swim the groove of serene.

In this sanctuary, the music's a play,
Where silence composes a jovial sway.
With friends gathered 'round, the giggles take flight,
Creating sweet chaos, our hearts feeling light.

The Thrum of Togetherness

In the kitchen, pots and pans,
Dancing like they're in a band.
The fridge hums a jaunty tune,
While the cat struts like a buffoon.

In the living room, a sock war,
Siblings giggle, then they soar.
Remote battles and popcorn fights,
This chaos sparks our wild delights.

Outside, the dog digs a hole,
Chasing tails is his main goal.
Neighbors peek and shake their heads,
While we laugh till we fall in beds.

In the bathroom, splashes abound,
The rubber ducky, its silly sound.
Squeaky toys and foam and fun,
Every act brings a smile, just one!

Sounds of the Sacred Spaces

In the hallway, echoes reign,
Footfalls dance like a train's refrain.
The walls are scribbles with laughter's grace,
Every corner holds a silly face.

In the den, the TV blares,
Comedy gold with wild affairs.
A pizza slice crashes on the floor,
We giggle like it's nothing more.

The laundry room's a twisty maze,
Mismatched socks in a wild craze.
Whirring washers sing out loud,
While we boogie like it's quite allowed.

Outside the window, squirrels bicker,
As we munch on snacks and snicker.
This cacophony of joy and glee,
Makes every space a home, you see!

The Unseen Embrace

Under the table, a hidden game,
A ticklish foot brings forth a name.
Sneaky giggles and whispered spells,
In this universe, hilarity dwells.

The attic's filled with dusty dreams,
Old toys whisper their wild schemes.
As we rummage through treasures rare,
A tumble leads to laughter's flare.

The porch swing creaks a flirty tune,
As we sway beneath the moon.
Daring dares and silly cheers,
Memories made throughout the years.

Each nook nested with love and jest,
Here's where we find our very best.
In this haven of joy and cheer,
Laughter tethers, drawing us near!

The Pulse of Familiarity

In the pantry, snacks on guard,
Chips and cookies, oh so hard!
A sprinkle of chaos in each bite,
Midst the laughs, our hearts feel light.

The dining table's set for fun,
Storytelling 'til the day is done.
Forks are swords, and napkins, capes,
We're all heroes, no need for scrapes.

The creek out back sings to the sky,
Where frogs pretend they can fly.
River rocks make the best of seats,
We chuckle at each frog's small feats.

With every room, our antics grow,
It's the laughter that lifts the glow.
Amidst the giggles we find our base,
In this wild, merry, beloved place!

www.ingramcontent.com/pod-product-compliance
Lightning Source LLC
Chambersburg PA
CBHW060110230426
43661CB00003B/136